PARENTING TIPS BY EXPERTS

INFORMATIVE QUOTES, SOOTHING AFFIRMATIONS & WITTY QUIPS ON PARENTING, MOTHERHOOD AND CHILDREN

SANJAY GORA

Made with ♥ on the Notion Press Platform
www.notionpress.com

Contents

Acknowledgements

This book is in your hands thanks to my daughter
Khushi Gora
(cover photo)
who inspired me to look for and compile these quotes in my quest to be
a better parent.
My life partner Archana Gora is my co-learner in this parenting
journey.

I
Quotes on Quotes

The obvious is that which is never seen until someone expresses it simply. (K Gibran)

If I have seen further it is by standing on the shoulders of giants. (Sir Isaac Newton)

It is a good thing for an educated man to read books of quotations. (Sir Winston Churchill)

It is a pleasure to be able to quote lines to fit any occasion. (Abraham Lincoln)

II
Parenting Tips by Experts

A child educated only at school is an uneducated child. (George Santayana)

A child enters your home and for the next twenty years makes so much noise you can hardly stand it. The child departs, leaving the house so silent you think you are going mad. (JA Holmes)

A child may not know what direction he is going, but when he is attached to you, he does not feel lost. (Gordon Neufeld)

A child who is not afraid to trigger their parent, likely feels secure in their relationship. (J Milburn)

A child with secure attachment always comes back to their attachment figure, at some point. Not because they feel obligated to, but because it is their home. (Anon)

A child, like your stomach, does not need all you can afford to give it. (Frank A Clark)

❧

A child's attempts at connection can feel like a deliberate effort to push your buttons. But when a child can't find an adult to connect with, they will keep signalling. (Patty Wipfler)

❧

A child's mind is not a container to be filled but rather a fire to be kindled. (D Brande)

❧

A child's behaviour we see on the surface is the reflection of the feelings that are rooted underneath. We can use topical treatments to try to shape what the behaviour looks like, but if we really want things to change, we need to address the roots. Nourish the roots, see the growth.(Kelly Bartlett)

❧

A dam doesn't try to reason with the water. Its main purpose is to hold it still for a while. When I lecture my kids I'm doing much the same thing. I'm not trying to necessarily reason with them, just hold them still for a short while. (Spuds Crawford)

❧

A dysregulated adult will never regulate a dysregulated child. (Dr Bruce Perry)

❧

A father carries pictures where his money used to be. (Steve Martin)

❧

A father is the man who can change a world he will not be part of by building the tiny human that is part of him. (Craig D Lounsbrough)

❧

A father is the man who teaches trembling hands to reach up in search of everything impossible, for he has left his child with the unbridled sense that to do anything less is the greatest impossibility of all. (Craig D Lounsbrough)

A good children's book is a conversation children and their parents share and talk about. (Suzy Davies)

❧

A good father is a source of inspiration and self-restraint. A good mother is the root of kindness and humbleness. (Dr TP Chia)

❧

A good mother loves fiercely but ultimately brings up her children to thrive without her. They must be the most important thing in her life, but if she is the most important thing in theirs, she has failed. (Erin Kelly)

❧

A good parent is not someone that knows how to be a good parent, but knows how to learn how to be a good parent. (Gary Edward Gedall)

❧

A lot of parents will do anything for their kids except let them be themselves. (Banksy)

❧

A mother is she who can take the place of all others, but whose place no one else can take. (Cardinal Mermillod)

❧

A mother understands what a child does not say. (Jewish Proverb)

❧

A mother's love is like an everlasting bed of roses that continues to blossom. A mother's love bears strength, comfort, healing and warmth. Her beauty is compared to a sunny day that shines upon each rose petal and inspires hope. (Ellen J Barrier)

❧

A parent is the compass carefully laid on the map of a child who has yet to understand that the present is nothing more than the place where the future begins, not the place where the future lives. (Craig D Lounsbrough)

A parent's love is whole no matter how many times divided. (Robert Brault)

A powerful phrase your child needs to hear every day : I love you, no matter what. (Carolina King)

A three-year-old child is a being who gets almost as much fun out of a fifty-six-dollar set of savings as it does out of finding a small green worm.
(Bill Vaughan)

A torn jacket is soon mended; but hard words bruise the heart of a child.
(HW Longfellow)

A yummy mummy is a dedicated and loving mom who embodies a healthy lifestyle while retaining a sense of the person she was before having kids.
(Marina Delio)

Adults who are respectful of children are not just modelling a skill or behaviour, they are meeting the emotional needs of those children, thereby helping to create the psychological conditions for children to treat others respectfully. (Alfie Kohn)

Affirming words from moms and dads are like light switches. Speak a word of affirmation at the right moment in a child's life and it is like lighting up a whole roomful of possibilities. (Gary Smalley)

All of us have moments in our lives that test our courage. Taking children into a house with a white carpet is one of them. (Erma Bombeck)

❧

All our children need is to feel loved. Love them much. Love them hard. Love them unconditionally, and make sure they know it. (Carolina King)

❧

All people cross the line from childhood to adulthood with a secondhand opinion of who they are. Without any questioning, we take as truth whatever our parents and other influentials have said about us during our childhood, whether these messages are communicated verbally, physically, or silently. (Heyward Ewart)

❧

All that I am, or hope to be, I owe to my mother. (Abraham Lincoln)

❧

Allow children to be happy in their own way, for what better way will they find? (Samuel Johnson)

❧

Always be nice to your children because they are the ones who will choose your rest home. (Phyllis Diller)

❧

24/7, once you sign on to be a mother, that is the only shift they offer. (Jodi Picoult)

❧

Always kiss your children goodnight, even if they are already asleep. (HJ Brown Jr)

❧

Americans are like a rich father who wishes he knew how to give his sons the hardships that made him rich. (Robert Frost)

❧

An adolescent does not rebel against his parents. He rebels against their power. If parents would rely less on power and more on non-power methods to influence their children from infancy on, there would be little for children to rebel against when they become adolescents. (Thomas Gordon)

And most of the failures in parent-child relationships, from my observation, begin when the child begins to acquire a mind and a will of its own, to make independent decisions and to question the omnipotence or the wisdom of the parent. (Sydney J. Harris)

❧

Anybody out there who is a parent, if your kids want to paint their bedrooms, as a favor to me, let them do it. It'll be OK. (Randy Pausch)

❧

Apologizing to your child does not undermine your authority or make you less in charge. It makes you a whole person : honest, accountable and reliable. (Dr Siggie)

❧

As a kid, I wanted to be a superhero, psychologist, philanthropist, philosopher,actor and comedian...so I became a teacher. (Anon)

❧

As a mother, you have that impulse to wish that no child should ever be hurt, or abused, or go hungry, or not have opportunities in life. (Annie Lennox)

❧

As a parent, you do have to constantly remind yourself that you are not a god, moulding a human in your own image. You are merely supporting whatever your child chooses to become, even if those choices don't always thrill you. (Heather Havrilesky)

❧

As parents we have a tendency to overprotect; it's okay to try and show them all positives but we cannot forget that the real world has teeth. (Johnnie Dent Jr)

❧

As the adults, we are the ones who set the stage for vitality, love, or disharmony in the home. We set ourselves up for one or the other, and our children take their cues from us. (Gabriel Cousens)

❧

Ask any child who failed to live up to his parents' idea of success, and you'll likely hear that they never felt good enough, or that their parents had expectations that they could not live up to. (Nancy Rose)

❧

Ask your child what he wants for dinner only if he is buying. (Fran Lebowitz)

❧

At the end of the day, the most overwhelming key to a child's success is the positive involvement of parents. (Jane D Hull)

❧

Bad moments don't make bad moms. (Lisa T)

❧

Balance is what it is all about no matter what your job is. Being a mom, working, and dividing your time. It is what we all have to do as mothers. (Carrie Underwood)

❧

Be careful to leave your sons well instructed rather than rich, for the hopes of the instructed are better than the wealth of the ignorant. (Epictetus)

❧

Because children grow up, we think a child's purpose is to grow up. But a child's purpose is to be a child. (Tom Stoppard)

❧

Because of their size, parents may be difficult to discipline properly. (PJ O'Rourke)

Because that was a parent's job: to provide shoulders. Shoulders for your children to sit on when they're little so they can see the world, then stand on when they get older so they can reach the clouds, and sometimes lean against whenever they stumble and feel unsure. They trust us, which is a crushing responsibility, because they haven't yet realised that we don't actually know what we're doing. (Fredrik Backman)

Become a foul weather friend to your child and deal in the currency of trust. (Ramendra Kumar)

Becoming a mom to me means that you have accepted that for the next 16 years of your life, you will have a sticky purse. (Nia Vardalos)

Becoming more aware of child development needs and risk factors can be a powerful motivation for promoting education, prevention, and recovery for ourselves as parents and our communities. (Mike Weiford)

Before I had kids, I always found it funny how people would talk about their children like they were the cutest things on the planet and how every little thing they did was endlessly fascinating. Now that I've had kids, I can say with certainty that my children really are the cutest things on this planet and every little thing they do is endlessly fascinating. (Jennifer Miller)

Before I married, I had three theories about raising children and no children. Now, I have three children and no theories. (John Wilnot)

Behind every young child who believes in himself is a parent who believed first. (Mathew L Jacobson)

❧

Being a father is the single greatest feeling on Earth. Not including those wonderful years I spent without a child, of course. (Ryan Reynolds)

❧

Being a good parent is not an obligation, it is a choice. Plenty of people fall short in the parent category and quite a few refuse to accept it. You will do a much better job if you understand that taking care of your children is a choice not an obligation. (Gudjon Bergmann)

❧

Being a mother can be like drying out the foundations of a house or mending a roof: it takes time, sweat, and money, and once it's done everything looks exactly the same as it did before. It's not the sort of thing anyone gives you praise for. But spending an extra hour in the office is like hanging up a beautiful painting or a new lamp: everyone notices. (Fredrik Backman)

❧

Being a mother is an attitude, not a biological relation. (Robert AH)

❧

Being a mother is learning about strengths you didn't know you had, and dealing with fears you didn't know existed. (Linda Wooten)

❧

Being a mother is not about what you gave up to have a child, but what you gained y having one. (Sunny Gupta)

❧

Being a parent is dirty and scary and beautiful and hard and miraculous and exhausting and thankless and joyful and frustrating all at once. It's everything. (Jill Smokler)

❧

Being a parent makes you feel like a blanket that is always too small. No matter how hard you try to cover everyone, there is always someone who is freezing. (Fredrik Backman)

❧

Being a perfectionist does not apply when it comes to children and a tidy house. (Renny Adejuwon)

❧

Blame or credit does not belong to the child alone. Parents, those who raised the child, must be given equal credit, or blame. That does not change, when the child is one, twenty or ninety years old. (Omar Kiam)

❧

But kids don't stay with you if you do it right. It is the one job where, the better you are, the more surely you won't be needed in the long run. (Barbara K)

❧

By loving them for more than their abilities we show our children that they are much more than the sum of their accomplishments. (Eileen KM)

❧

Checking in on what our kids are doing online isn't 'helicoptering,' it's 'parenting'. (Galit Breen)

❧

Childhood serves a purpose ; It is not something to get through or speed up. It is there to protect developing minds. To nurture young souls.So, let us give our kids the space to be unbusy. Let us unschedule. Let us miss out.Let us hold the space for childhood. Because childhood is not a dress rehearsal for adulthood.(Tracy Gillett)

❧

Children are educated by what the grown-up is and not by his talk. (Carl Jung)

❧

Children are gifts. They are not ours for the breaking. They are ours for the making. (Dan Pearce)

☙

Children are made readers on the lap of their parents. (Emilie Buchwald)

☙

Children are mirrors; they will always show you exactly what is going on inside of you. Each phase of their growth is an opportunity to heal your own pain, to go deeper inside yourself and become more truly human. (Vimala McClure)

☙

Children are not a distraction from more important work, they are the most important work. (CS Lewis)

☙

Children are our second chance to have a great parent-child relationship. (Laura S)

☙

Children are people, and they should have to reach to learn about things, to understand things, just as adults have to reach if they want to grow in mental stature. (Walt Disney)

☙

Children are souls to be nurtured, not products to be measured. (Andrew Kern)

☙

Children begin by loving their parents; as they grow older they judge them; sometimes they forgive them. (Oscar Wilde)

☙

Children behave how they feel. (Lelia Schott)

☙

Children do not enter this world with bad intentions. They do not come to wear us out, test our patience, or push us over the edge. They come to us with a need for love, connection and belonging. (Rebecca Eanes)

❦

Children do not need to learn how to handle separation. Instead they need to develop the ability to hold on when apart. (Gordon Neufeld)

❦

Children don't need you to be the best reader, just a willing one. (Jacqui Shepherd)

❦

Children don't say "I had a hard day. Can we talk?" They say "Will you play with me?" (Lawrence Cohen)

❦

Children harbor a great many doubts and sorrows that could be eased by a loving hug from a parent.(Richelle E. Goodrich)

❦

Children have deep devotion to life and this devotion is beautifully expressed through free play. Objects of play should be as simple as possible, to allow the power of imagination to flourish. Buying 'perfect', expensive toys, rob the children of an ability to see beauty in a stone or a shell. (Natasa Pantovic Nuit)

❦

Children have more need of models than of critics. (Carolyn Coats)

❦

Children have never been very good at listening to their elders, but they have never failed to imitate them. (James Baldwin)

❦

Children learn best when they like their teacher and they think their teacher likes them. (Gordon Neufeld)

❦

Children learn by doing and doing is noisy, untidy, messy and unpredictable. (Anon)

❧

Children learn from anything and everything they see. They learn wherever they are, not just in special learning places. (John Holt)

❧

Children must be taught how to think, not what to think. (Margaret Mead)

❧

Children must never work for our love ; they must rest in it. (Dr Gordon Neufeld)

❧

Children need at least one person in their life that thinks the sun rises and sets on them, who delights in their existence, and loves them unconditionally. (Pamela Leo)

❧

Children require guidance and sympathy far more than instruction. (Anne SM)

❧

Children should learn that reading is a pleasure, not just something that teachers make you do in school. (Beverly Cleary)

❧

Children should not be burdened with making us happy, nor blamed for making us sad or angry. Children are not responsible for how we feel. We are.(Larissa Dann)

❧

Children should not be taught to get a job or pursue a profession. Children should be taught to discover their passion and with it define their mission. (Tarryn Tomlinson)

❧

Children that have been abused do not have behaviour problems that need to be addressed. They have extreme survival skills that need to be understood. (Paula Goodwin)

Children who have faith have distinctly different characteristics from those who don't. In fact, one of the main manifestations of a person with strong faith is the ability to give—not just in terms of money or possessions, but also time, love, and encouragement. (Stormie Omartian)

Children will discover their passions...if only they are given the time to do so. (Shelby Dersa)

Children will not remember you for the material things you provided but for the feeling that you cherished them. (RL Evans)

Children's achievements are not status symbols for parents. As a parent, your job is to support kids in pursuing their own goals, not push them toward yours. The key question is not what accomplishment will reflect best on you - it's what activity will best build their character. (Adam Grant)

Children's imaginations are too often killed by embarrassed parents. (Darnell Lamont Walker)

Cleaning your house while your kids are still growing up is like shovelling the walk before it stops snowing. (Phillys Diller)

Curiosity is more important than knowledge. (Albert Einstein)

Dad needs to show an incredible amount of respect and humor and friendship toward his mate so the kids understand their parents are sexy, they are fun, they do things together, they are best friends. Kids learn by example. If I respect Mom, they are going to respect Mom. (Tim Allen)

৪৩

Dietary patterns are set at a very early age—somewhere between four and eight years old. The research shows that children who have established a healthy diet are healthier in the longer range and less likely to develop cancer, heart disease, stroke, diabetes, and obesity.(Gabriel Cousens)

৪৩

Do not let a broken system convince you that you have a broken child. (Anon)

৪৩

Do not trash your child's little proposals, suggestions and her tiny dreams. They may not be important to you, but they mean a whole world to her. (Ramendra Kumar)

৪৩

Don't force your children into your ways, for they were created for a time different from your own. (Plato)

৪৩

Don't handicap your children by making their lives easy. (Robert AH)

৪৩

Don't just teach your children to read...Teach them to question what they read. Teach them to question everything. (George Carlin)

৪৩

Don't let yourself become so concerned with raising a good kid that you forget you already have one. (Glennon Doyle)

৪৩

Don't make any parenting decisions when you are feeling angry as anger clouds your judgement. When in doubt ask yourself "What would love do?"

(Carolina King)

ॐ

Don't worry that children never listen to you, worry that they are always watching you. (Robert Fulghum)

ॐ

Don't get too involved in your children's lives. Don't tell your kids what to do; just foster the right worldview in them so that they will choose to do the right things. (Leila Sales)

ॐ

Don't just teach your kids, train them how to learn from everything. (Dido Stargaze)

ॐ

Don't try to make children grow up to be like you, or they may do it. (Russell Baker)

ॐ

During childhood, it's about trying to help develop who your kid's going to be. During adolescence, it's about responding to who your kid wants to be. (Jennifer Senior)

ॐ

Each day of our lives we make deposits in the memory banks of our children. (Charles R Swindoll)

ॐ

Educate the children and it won't be necessary to punish the men. (Pythagoras)

ॐ

Educate your children to self-control, to the habit of holding passion and prejudice and evil tendencies subject to an upright and reasoning will, and you have done much to abolish misery from their future and crimes from society. (Benjamin Franklin)

ॐ

Education is not something you can finish. (Isaac Asimov)

❧

Encourage and support your kids because children are apt to live up to what you believe in them. (LB Johnson)

❧

Encourage kindness in children by showing them, with your actions, what kindness looks like. (Carolina King)

❧

Enjoy the little things, for one day you may look back and realize they were the big things. (Robert Brault)

❧

Even as kids reach adolescence, they need more than ever for us to watch over them. Adolescence is not about letting go. It is about hanging on during a very bumpy ride. (Ron Taffel)

❧

Every child deserves a champion- an adult who will never give up on them, who understands the power of connection and insists that they become the best that they can possibly be. (Rita Pierson)

❧

Every child is an artist until he is told he is not an artist. (John Lennon)

❧

Every child is gifted. They just unwrap their packages at different times. (Anon)

❧

Every day, in a hundred small ways our children ask, "Do you hear me? Do you see me? Do I matter?" Their behaviour often reflects our response. (LR Knost)

❧

Every mama knows what is best for her child, if she truly listens to what her heart is saying. (Carolina King)

৪৩

Every parent is an artist, but not every artist is apparent. (Eric Micha'el Leventhal)

৪৩

Every parent is an artist, for the bared canvas of a newborn's soul begs for the artist's touch. And because this is so, a parent must prepare the palette with the utmost care, choose the brushes with poised caution, and mindfully attend to every brushstroke regardless of how slight. And such caution is utterly imperative for the emerging rendering will be both a legacy borne by the parent, and a life lived by the child. (Craig D. Lounsbrough)

৪৩

Everybody knows how to raise children except the people who have them. (PJ O'Rourke)

৪৩

Everyone who remembers his own education remembers teachers, not methods and techniques. The teacher is the heart of the educational system. (Sidney Hook)

৪৩

Everything depends on upbringing. (Leo Tolstoy)

৪৩

Father has a strengthening character like the sun and mother has a soothing temper like the moon. (Amit Kalantri)

৪৩

Fatherhood is important to me. I've taught my daughter to cherish nature, to nurture her spirituality, to love herself, to love others, to explore science, and to seek wisdom and understanding. I make it a point to cultivate those things in her, in the way that only a father can. (Hendrith Vanlon Smith Jr)

৪৩

For me, being a mother made me a better professional, because coming home every night to my girls reminded me what I was working for. And being a professional made me a better mother, because by pursuing my dreams, I was modelling for my girls how to pursue their dreams. (Michelle Obama)

ॐ

Free the child's potential, and you will transform him into the world. (Maria Montessori)

ॐ

Fussing over children who cry only encourages them. That's positive reinforcement for negative behaviour. (Jeannette Walls)

ॐ

Genuine love for a child, it seems to me, must include a desire for his maturity and ultimately his independence. Watching a personality unfold is perhaps the deepest pleasure of parenthood; wishing, or trying, to retard this growth is one of the deepest sins. (Sydney J Harris)

ॐ

Get to know your child, learn about alternative parenting ways, listen to your intuition and parent them the way it feels right to you. (Carolina King)

ॐ

Girls are the future mothers of our society, and it is important that we focus on their wellbeing. (Miriam Makeba)

ॐ

Give the ones you love wings to fly, roots to come back and reasons to stay. (Dalai Lama)

ॐ

Give your children regular, daily doses of Vitamin N. This vital nutrient consists simply of the most character-building two-letter word in the English language NO. (John Rosemond)

ॐ

God, why does a mortal man have children? It is senseless to love anything this much. (Barbara K)

Good parenting is not about fulfilling the dreams of the parents, it is about helping the children become strong and conscientious human beings so that they can achieve their dreams. (Abhijit Naskar)

Good parents hardly parent. They let their kids learn, fail and grow without interference. (Trevor Carss)

Having a baby dragged me, kicking and screaming, from the world of self-absorption. (Paul Reiser)

Having a baby is a life-changer. It gives you a whole other perspective on why you wake up every day. (Taylor Hanson)

Having a child flips your concept of love upside down into new depths, otherwise unknown to the human heart. (J O'Connor)

Having children is like living in a frat house- nobody sleeps, everything is broken, and there is a lot of throwing up. (Ray Romano)

Having kids - the responsibility of rearing good, kind, ethical, responsible human beings- is the biggest job anyone can embark on. As with any risk, you have to take a leap of faith and ask lots of wonderful people for their help and guidance. I thank God every day for giving me the opportunity to parent. (Maria Shriver)

Helping your child fulfil her true potential should be your ultimate goal as a parent.(Ramendra Kumar)

❧

Hey, great idea : if you have kids, give your partner reading vouchers next Christmas. Each voucher entitles the bearer to two hours' reading time while the kids are awake. It might look like a cheapskate present, but parents will appreciate that it costs more in real terms than a Lamborghini. (Nick Hornby)

❧

I am a mother. I see clearly that while I've been teaching them, they have been my reason to learn. (Tsara Shelton)

❧

I am beginning to perceive motherhood as a long, slow letting go, of which birth is just the first step. (Sandra Steingraber)

❧

I am not a parenting expert. In fact, I am not sure that I even believe in the idea of parenting experts. I am an engaged, imperfect, parent and a passionate researcher. I am an experienced mapmaker and a stumbling traveller. Like many of you, parenting is by far my boldest and mst daring adventure. (Brene Brown)

❧

I am so cool that the kids come to my bedroom and go, "Mom, turn the music down." (Melissa Etheridge)

❧

I am the exact parent my child needs to blossom, so I don't need to compare myself to others. (Lauren Tamm)

❧

I became the kind of parent my mother was to me. (Maya Angelou)

❧

I began to see that he was flawed. We are all flawed, but it is a powerful moment when you realise that about your parents. Still, I loved him no less for it. I know I have flaws, and my children are free to realise this and make their own corrections. (Ziauddin Yousafzai)

❧

I believe that what we become depends on what our fathers teach us at odd moments, when they are not trying to teach us. We are formed by little scraps of wisdom. (Umberto Eco)

❧

I came to parenting the way most of us do-knowing nothing and trying to learn everything. (Mayim B)

❧

I do think that there is an art form to parenting, and I have nothing but admiration for those who do it well. (Elizabeth Berg)

❧

I don't know what is more exhausting about parenting : the getting up early, or acting like you know what you are doing. (Jim Gaffigan)

❧

I don't remember who said this, but there really are places in the heart you don't even know exist until you love a child. (Anne Lamott)

❧

I don't think it matters how many parents you have got, as long as those who are around make their presence a good one. (Elizabeth Wurtzel)

❧

I don't think it really matters whether parents are strict or lenient, as long as they're consistent. Kids can live with more or less any set of rules so long as they know what they are. It's arbitrary tyranny that gets them mixed up. (Ken Follett)

❧

I don't want my kids to be like me. I want them to be better than me.
(Katherine Center)

ಇ

I feel very blessed to have two wonderful, healthy children who keep me completely grounded, sane and throw up on my shoes just before I go to an awards show just so I know to keep it real. (Reese Witherspoon)

ಇ

I give you my hand, I give you my soul, I am your trustee, Can I be your bestie ! (Vasantha K Dandem)

ಇ

I have three daughters, so I can't be as tough as I want to be. When you have kids-especially daughters-they know how to work you. They are a lot smarter than we are, that is for sure.But I will be more tough on their boyfriends. (Tim Mcgraw)

ಇ

I just want my kids to love who they are, have happy lives and find some thing they want to do and make peace with that. Your job as a parent is to give your kids not only the instincts and talents to survive, but help them enjoy their lives. (Susan Sarandon)

ಇ

I love how teenagers just be planning stuff. No money. No ride. No permission. No nothing. Just planning. (Anon)

ಇ

I love my children beyond all reason. They are my joy, even when they are wild with kid energy. (Christopher Meloni)

ಇ

I love my mother as trees love water and sunshine. She helps me grow, prosper, and reach great heights. (Terry G)

ಇ

I may not be able to give my kids everything they want, but I give them what they need: love, time, and attention. You can't buy those things. (Nishan Panwar)

৪৩

I prefer peace. But if trouble must come, let it come in my time, so that my children can live in peace. (Thomas Paine)

৪৩

I think that's the problem. Teenagers think their parents should have it all figured out, but the truth is, adults don't really know how to navigate life any better than teenagers do. (Colleen Hoover)

৪৩

I want my children to have all the things I couldn't afford. Then I want to move in with them. (Phyllis Diller)

৪৩

I want them to see a mother who loves them dearly, who invests in them, but who also invests in herself. It is just as much about letting them know as young women that it is okay to put yourself a little higher on your priority list. (Michelle Obama)

৪৩

I wish you would moderate that fondness you have for your children. I do not mean you should abate any part of your care, or not do your duty to them in its utmost extent, but I would have you early prepare yourself for disappointments, which are heavy in proportion to their being surprising. (MW Montagu)

৪৩

I would teach children music, physics and philosophy ; but most importantly music, for the patterns in music and all the arts are the keys to learning. (Plato)

৪৩

If a child gets lots of partial, halfhearted attention from you most of the time but gets your undivided attention when she acts up, chances are she will act up. (Susan Stiffelman)

☙

If a child is poor in math but good at tennis, most people would hire a math tutor. I would rather hire a tennis coach. (Deepak Chopra)

☙

If a child lives with acceptance and friendship, he learns to find love in the world. (Dorothy Nolte)

☙

If all we ever offer is blanket praise without any meaning behind it, kids will always seek approval because they'll never feel satisfied. If we offer genuine encouragement for their accomplishments, they won't need our approval; they'll approve of themselves. (Kelly Bartlett)

☙

If I feel good about my parenting, I have no interest in judging other people's choices. If I feel good about my body, I don't go around making fun of other people's weight or appearance. We are hard on each other because we are using each other as a launching pad out of our own perceived deficiency. (Brene Brown)

☙

If I had my child to raise all over again, I would finger paint more, and point the finger less. I would do less correcting, and more connecting. I would take my eyes off my watch, and watch with my eyes. I would care to know less, and know to care more. I would take more hikes and fly more kites. I would stop playing serious, and seriously play. I would run through more fields, and gaze at more stars. I would do more hugging, and less tugging. I would be firm less often, and affirm much more. I would build self-esteem first, and the house later. I would teach less about the love of power, and more about the power of love. (Diana Loomans)

☙

If I had to make a general rule for living and working with children , it might be this; be wary of saying or doing anything to a child that you would not do to another adult, whose good opinion and affection you valued. (John Holt)

∞

If John Lennon was right that life is what happens when you are making other plans, parenthood is what happens when everything is flipped over and spilling everywhere and you can't find a towel or a sponge or your inside voice. (Kelly Corrigan)

∞

If our children were to grow up truthful they must be taught by those who had a regard for truth, and not just a casual record, a delicate regard. On this point we were adamant. (Amy Carmichael)

∞

If parents want to give their children a gift, the best thing they can do is to teach their children to love challenges, be intrigued by mistakes, enjoy effort, and keep on learning. That way, their children don't have to be slaves of praise. They will have a lifelong way to build and repair their own confidence. (Carol S. Dweck)

∞

If the day ever came when we were able to accept ourselves and our children exactly as we and they are, then, I believe, we would have come very close to an ultimate understanding of what good parenting means. (Fred Rogers)

∞

If the people around you can't hold space for the glorious magic of a child, why are you trying to appease them? Never apologise for the presence of your children. Do not look to calm the insecurities of others. (Amethyst Joy)

∞

If the sound of happy children is grating on your ears, I don't think it is the children who need to be adjusted. (Stefan Molyneux)

∞

If there is anything that we wish to change in the child, we should first examine it and see whether it is not something that could better be changed in ourselves. (Carl Jung)

೫

If there were three character traits that I would recommend for my children to cultivate, they would be perseverance, logical thinking and empathy. (NB Godrej)

೫

If we are to hope for a society of culturally literate people, music must be a vital part of our children's education. (Yo-yo Ma)

೫

If we are wonderful parents and family members, then there's really nothing else to prove. (Ron Baratono)

೫

If we can relax when our strong emotions come, then we don't pass fear to our children and to future generations. (Thich Nhat Hanh)

೫

If we don't shape our kids, they will be shaped by outside forces that don't care what shape our kids are in. (Dr. Louise Hart)

೫

If we never have headaches through rebuking our children, we shall have plenty of heartaches when they grow up. (Charles H Spurgeon)

೫

If we teach a child to read but fail to develop a desire to read, we will have created a skilled nonreader, a literate illiterate, and no high test score will ever undo that damage. (Kylene Beers)

೫

If you are a parent, open doors to unknown directions to the child so he can explore. Don't make him afraid of the unknown,give him support. (Osho)

೫

If you are able to talk about your life and the joys and sorrows you have experienced, if you know your story, you are much more likely to be a skillful parent. (Desmond Tutu)

☙

If you bungle raising your children, I don't think whatever else you do matters very much. (Jackie Kennedy)

☙

If you can control your behaviour when everything around you is out of control, you can model for your children a valuable lesson in patience and understanding. (Jane CJ)

☙

If you can give your son or daughter only one gift, let it be enthusiasm. (Bruce Barton)

☙

If you don't teach your children to be alone, they will only know how to be lonely. (Anon)

☙

If you have never been hated by your child, you have never been a parent. (Bette Davis)

☙

If you raise your children to feel that they can accomplish any goal or task they decide upon, you will have succeeded as a parent and you will have given your children the greatest of blessings. (Brian Tracy)

☙

If you trust play, you will not have to control your child's development as much. Play will raise the child in ways you can never imagine. (Vince Gowman)

☙

If you want children to keep their feet on the ground, put some responsibility on their shoulders. (AV Buren)

ॐ

If you want kids, choose your girlfriend like your future child has the deciding vote. (Stefan Molyneux)

ॐ

If you want to know what God thinks about any situation in the world, think like a parent. (Suzy Kassem)

ॐ

If you want to love a parent you have to understand the incredible investment he or she has in you. If you are a parent, and you want to be loved, you have to deserve it. (Jodi Picoult)

ॐ

If you want your children to improve, let them overhear the nice things you say about them to others. (H Ginott)

ॐ

If you want your children to turn out well, spend twice as much time with them, and half as much money. (Abigail Van Buren)

ॐ

If your child feels loved, they feel safe. If your child feels loved, they can open up to you. If your child feels loved, they will be courageous in life because they know they have a cushion to fall back on. If there is one big gift we can give our children is to know they are truly loved, no matter what. (Carolina King)

ॐ

If your children fear you, they cannot trust you. If they don't trust you, they cannot learn from you. (Lori Petro)

ॐ

If your kid needs a role model and you ain't it, you are both fucked. (George Carlin)

ॐ

If your kids are giving you a headache, follow the directions on the aspirin bottle, especially the part that says, keep away from children. (Susan Savannah)

☙

If your parents' faces never lit up when they looked at you, it's hard to know what it feels like to be loved and cherished. If you come from an incomprehensible world filled with secrecy and fear, it's almost impossible to find the words to express what you have endured. If you grew up unwanted and ignored, it is a major challenge to develop a visceral sense of agency and self-worth. (Bessel A van der Kolk)

☙

If you're not parenting on purpose, don't be surprised when you get chaos from the children. (Benjamin Lotter)

☙

In automobile terms, the child supplies the power but the parents have to do the steering. (Benjamin Spock)

☙

In the United States today, there is a pervasive tendency to treat children as adults, and adults as children. The options of children are thus steadily expanded, while those of adults are progressively constricted. The result is unruly children and childish adults. (Thomas Stephen Szasz)

☙

Insanity is hereditary. You can get it from your children. (Sam Levenson)

☙

Instant availability without continuous presence is probably the best role a mother can play. (Lotte Bailyn)

☙

Instead of buying your children all the things you never had, you should teach them all the things you were never taught. Materials wears out but knowledge stays. (Bruce Lee)

☙

Instead of training children to meet the expectations of adults, we should be training adults to meet the psychological, emotional and development needs of children. (Zoe Tolman)

છ

Instead of treating your child like how you were treated. Treat them with the same love and attention you wanted from your parents while growing up.(Jonathan Anthony Burkett)

છ

Instruction is good for a child, but an example is worth more. (Alexander Dumas)

છ

Ironically, to my children, bedtime is a punishment that violates their basic rights as human beings. Once the lights are out, you can expect at least an hour of inmates clanging their tin cups on the cell bars. (Jim Gaffigan)

છ

It goes without saying that you should never have more children than you have car windows. (Erma Bombeck)

છ

It is a great mistake, I think, to put children off with falsehoods and nonsense, when their growing powers observation and discrimination excite in them a desire to know about things. (Anne Sullivan Macy)

છ

It is a violation of trust to use your kids as caulking for the cracks in you. (Anne Lamott)

છ

It is amazing how quickly the kids learn to drive a car, yet are unable to understand the lawn mower, snowblower and vacuum cleaner. (Ben Berger)

છ

It is easier to build strong children than to repair broken men. (Frederick Douglas)

It is humbling to be the parent of a child who brings our all of your weaknesses repetitively. But living in guilt for not being perfect will never serve our need to grow stronger. (Sally Clarkson)

It is impossible to protect your kids against disappointment in life. (Nicholas Sparks)

It is my pleasure that my children are free and happy, and unrestrained by parental tyranny. Love is the chain whereby to bind a child to its parents. (Abraham Lincoln)

It is never ok to punish a child for exasperating behaviour that is due entirely to underdeveloped brain systems. (Dr. Margot Sunderland)

It is not a church's job to spiritually develop your children. Scripturally, it is the job of the parents. The church body is supposed to support parents in raising children, not replace them. (George Barna)

It is not difficult to take care of a child, it is difficult to do anything else while taking care of a child. (Julianne Moore)

It is not only children who grow. Parents do too. As much as we watch to see what our children do with their lives, they are watching us to see what we do with ours. I can't tell my children to reach for the sun. All I can do is reach for it, myself. (Joyce Maynard)

It is not our job to toughen our children up to face a cruel and heartless world. It is our job to raise children who will make the world a little less cruel and heartless. (LR Knost)

It is not the child's responsibility to make life easier for the adult, it is the adult's responsibility to make life easier for the child. (Rachel Sampson)

It is not what you leave to your children that matters, but what you leave in them. (Shannon L. Alder)

It is so awful, attacking your child. It is the worse thing I know, to shout loudly at this 50 lb. being with his huge trusting brown eyes. It is like bitch-slapping E.T. (Anne Lamott)

It is such a privilege to learn from children as they discover new worlds of possibility and give them selves full over to their dreams, inspiring a few adults along the way. (Colleen Mariotti)

It is the sunlight of parental love and encouragement that enables a child to grow in competence and slowly gain mastery over his environment.(Felicity Bauer)

It is time for parents to teach young people that in diversity there is beauty and there is strength.(Maya Angelou)

It just occurred to me that the majority of my diet is made up of the foods that my kid did not finish. (Carrie Underwood)

It kills you to see them grow up. But I guess it would kill you quicker if they did not. (Barbara K)

ೞ

It should not matter how slowly a child learns as long as we are encouraging them not to stop. ((RJ Meehan)

ೞ

It should not matter how slowly a child learns as long as we are encouraging them not to stop. (RJ Meehan)

ೞ

It would be easy to be a parent if you said yes all the time and gave them what they wanted, but you just can't do that. There are certain things, of course, where you are going to say no and be tougher on. (Chrissy Teigen)

ೞ

It's not an easy time for any parent, this moment when the realisation dawns that you've given birth to something that will never see things the way you do, despite the fact that it is your living legacy, that it bears your name. (Richard Russo)

ೞ

It's so important for husbands and wives to be united when making parenting decisions. If either parent doesn't feel good about something, then permission should not be granted. If either feels uncomfortable about a movie, a television show, a video game, a party, a dress, a swimsuit, or an Internet activity, have the courage to support each other and say no. (Larry R. Lawrence)

ೞ

It's not only children who grow. Parents do too. As much as we watch to see what our children do with their lives, they are watching us to see what we do with ours. I can't tell my children to reach for the sun. All I can do is reach for it, myself. (Joyce Maynard)

ೞ

Jokes about butts WORKED. (Drew Magary)

ೞ

Just because you are a parent does not mean your needs are not important. (Hilary Duff)

৪৩

Keeping inside all emotions will add up to your stress. Throw them all out at once, we will help you clear the mess. (Vasantha K Dandem)

৪৩

Kids. They're not easy. But there has to be some penalty for sex. (Bill Maher)

৪৩

Learning can only happen when a child is interested. If he is not interested, it is like throwing marshmallows at his head and calling it eating. (Katrina Gutleben)

৪৩

Leave your pride, ego and narcissism somewhere else. Reactions from those parts of you will reinforce your children's most primitive fears. (Henry Cloud)

৪৩

Let a child bear the truth, and sometimes fear it. Let him obtain nothing by flying into passion : let him be given when he is quiet what was refused when he cried for it. (Seneca)

৪৩

Life affords no greater responsibility, no greater privilege, than the raising of the next generation. (CE Koop)

৪৩

Listen earnestly to anything your children want to tell you, no matter what. If you don't listen eagerly to the little stuff when they are little, they won't tell you the big stuff when they are big, because to them all of it has always been big stuff. (Catherine M Wallace)

৪৩

Listen to the desires of your children. Encourage them and then give them the autonomy to make their own decision. (Denis Waitley)

�❧

Live so that when your children think of fairness, caring and integrity, they think of you. (HJ Brown Jr)

�❧

Love is staying up all night with a sick child or a healthy adult. (David Frost)

�❧

Love is the chain whereby to bind a child to its parents. (Abraham Lincoln)

�❧

Loving a child does not mean giving in to all his whims, to love him is to bring out the best in him, to teach him to love what is difficult. (Nadia Boulanger)

�❧

Making the decision to have a baby is momentous. It is to decide forever to have your heart go walking around outside of your body. (Elizabeth Stone)

�❧

Many believe that parenting is about controlling children's behaviour and training them to act like adults. I believe that parenting is about controlling my own behaviour and acting like an adult myself. Children learn what they live and live what they learn. (LR Knost)

�❧

Many men have children, but not many children have 'Fathers'. Age releases to you reproductive skills. Fatherhood requires leadership skills. (Fela Durotoye)

�❧

Men are what their mothers made them. (RW Emerson)

�❧

Misbehaviour and punishment are not opposites that cancel each other - on the contrary they breed and reinforce each other. (Haim G Ginott)

�❧

Morality in general is well enough known by men, but the particular refinements of virtue are unknown by most persons; thus the majority of parents, without knowing it and without intending it, give very bad examples to their children.(Anne RobeSome)

ം

Most American children suffer too much mother and too little father. (Gloria Steinem)

ം

Most children threaten at times to run away from home. This is the only thing that keeps some parents going. (Phyllis Diller)

ം

Most of our childhood is stored not in photos, but in certain biscuits, lights of day, smells, textures of carpet. (Alain de Botton)

ം

Most things are good, and they are the strongest things ; but there are evil things too, and you are not doing a child a favour by trying to shield him from reality. The important thing is to teach a child that good can always triumph over evil. (Walt Disney)

ം

Mother is a verb. It is something you do. Not just who you are. (Dorothy CF)

ം

Motherhood has completely changed me. It is just about like the most completely humbling experience that I have ever had. I think that it puts you in your place because it really focuses you to address the issues that you claim to believe in and if you can't stand up to those principles when you are raising a child, forget it. (Diane Keaton)

ം

Motherhood has taught me the meaning of living in the moment and being at peace. Children don't think about yesterday, and they don't think about tomorrow. They just exist in the moment. (Jessalyn Gilsig)

Motherhood is a glorious gift, but do not define yourself solely by motherhood. Be a full person. Your child will benefit from that. (CN Adichie)

Motherhood is like planting a garden; you tend and toil not to create the greatest bloom, but to keep the weeds and pests from destroying your crop. (Allene V)

Motherhood is putting the same 7 objects away 30 times a day. (Anon)

Mothers are the ultimate executives. Instead of raising profits they are raising humanity. (Virginia Burgess)

My advice to new moms is this : You have never been a mom before, and your baby is new to this world. So be kind to yourself, and be patient. It takes time, but you will get the hang of it. (Hillary Clinton)

My child is not my easel to paint on. Nor my diamond to polish. My child is not my trophy to share with the world. Not my badge of honour. My child is not an idea, and expectation, or a fantasy. (Dr Shefali Tsabury)

My children are the reason I laugh, smile and want to get up every morning. (GL Nolin)

My doctors told me I would never walk again. My mother told me I would. I believed my mother. (Wilma Rudolph)

My father didn't tell me how to live; he lived, and let me watch him do it.(Clarence Budinton Kelland)

❧

My father gave me the greatest gift anyone could give another person, he believed in me. (Jim Valvano)

❧

My heroes are and were my parents. I can't see having anyone else as my heroes. (Michael Jordan)

❧

My kid, her life. I want for her what she wants for herself. (Laura Castoro)

❧

My parents loved us but I wasn't always sure they liked us. (Tahereh Maf)

❧

My parents taught me I could be anything in the world I wanted to be. (Joan Jett)

❧

My work makes me a better mom. It gives me a little door to step out of my parenting and bring the excitement from my day back home. (Christie Brinkley)

❧

My worst parenting moments, the ones I am least proud of, happened because I was trying to impress a bunch of strangers I will probably never see again. (Janel Mills)

❧

Never fear spoiling children by making them too happy. Happiness is the atmosphere in which all good affections grow. (Thomas Bray)

❧

Never lend your car to anyone to whom you have given birth. (Erma Bombeck)

❦

No blade can puncture the human heart like the well-chosen words of a spiteful son. (Abraham Verghese)

❦

No career is final, choices are many, it's never too late to make enough money. Interest is 'in' and passion is the 'key'. Life is very generous, you need no worry. (Vasantha K Dandem)

❦

No man wants his daughter to be the kind of girl whom he liked in high school. (J Richard Singleton)

❦

No man, should bring children into the world, who is unwilling to persevere to the end in their nature and education. (Plato)

❦

No matter how calmly you try to referee, parenting will eventually produce bizarre behaviour, and I'm not talking about the kids. Their behaviour is always normal. (Bill Cosby)

❦

No matter how far we come, our parents are always in us. (Brad Meltzer)

❦

No matter how much time you spend reading books or following your intuition, you are gonna screw it up. Fifty times. You can't do parenting right. (Alan Arkin)

❦

No one is ever quite ready, everyone is always caught off guard. Parenthood chooses you. And you open your eyes, look at what you have got, say Oh my gosh, and recognise that of all the balls there ever were, this is the one you should not drop. It is not a question of choice. (Marisa D Santos)

No one knows his true character until he has run out of gas, purchased something on the instalment plan and raised an adolescent. (M Cox)

Nothing has a stronger influence psychologically on their environment and especially on their children than the unlived life of the parent. (Carl Jung)

Nothing should intrude into family time and the parent-child communication should be a sacrosanct activity. (Ramendra Kumar)

Nurturing a child's sense of personal worth and therefore hope and dreams for a wonderful future is perhaps the most important responsibility of every grownup in a child's life. (Wess Stafford)

Nurturing never happens in a rush. (Emma Scheib)

Of course, everyone's parents are embarrassing. It goes with the territory. The nature of parents is to embarrass merely by existing, just as it is the nature of children of a certain age to cringe with embarrassment, shame, and mortification should their parents so much as speak to them on the street. (Neil Gaiman)

On our 6 AM walk, my daughter asked where the moon goes each morning. I let her know it is in heaven, visiting daddy's freedom. (Ryan Reynolds)

One day ask your daughter the kind of mother she wants to be! One day ask your son the kind of father he wants to be! One day ask yourself the kind of parent you have been! And one day, ask yourself how you have run the race of life through the good and the bad times with the baton of life in your hands! (Ernest Agyemang Yeboah)

One doesn't need a correspondence course to appreciate the humorous side of things – all one needs is a fresh vision. (Ramendra Kumar)

෧

One hundred years from now it won't matter what your bank account was, the sort of house you lived in, or the kind of car you drove, but the world may be different because you were important in the life of a child. (FE Witcraft)

෧

One of the greatest problems of our time is that many are schooled but few are educated. (Thomas More)

෧

One of the most important gifts a parent can give a child is the gift of accepting that child's uniqueness. (Fred Rogers)

෧

One reason we have children I think is to learn that parts of ourselves we had given up for dead are merely dormant and that the old joys can re emerge fresh and new and in a completely different form. (Anne Fadiman)

෧

One reason we have children I think is to learn that parts of ourselves we had given up for dead are merely dormant and that the old joys can re emerge fresh and new and in a completely different form. (Anne Fadiman)

෧

One thing I had learned from watching chimpanzees with their infants is that having a child should be fun. (Jane Goodall)

෧

Our children are only as brilliant as we allow them to be. (Eric ML)

෧

Our children help us become aware of places inside of us that need healing. (Anon)

෧

Our generation of deeply loving parents would change the brain of the next generation, and with that, the world. (Charles Raison)

☙

Our greatest duty to our children is to love them first. Secondly, it is to teach them. Not to frighten, force, or intimidate our children into submission, but to effectively teach them so that they have the knowledge and tools to govern themselves. (Richelle E Goodrich)

☙

Parent time is magic : Down tempo and supersonic all at once, witch's time, sorcerer hours. Suddenly, while you are not paying attention, everything is changed. (Laurie Frankel)

☙

Parental Alienation is an emotional act of violence that is aimed at an adult, but critically wounds a child. (Steve Maraboli)

☙

Parenthood is about guiding the next generation and forgiving the last. (Peter Krause)

☙

Parenthood is above all a relationship, not a skill to be acquired. Attachment is not a behaviour to be learned , but a connection to be sought. (Neufeld & Mate)

☙

Parenthood is the opiate of the masses. (Chuck Palahniuk)

☙

Parenting and family life can be a perfect field for mindfulness practice, but it's not for the weak-hearted, the selfish or lazy, or the hopelessly romantic. Parenting is a mirror that forces you to look at yourself. If you can learn from what you observe, you just may have a chance to keep growing yourself. (Jon Kabat-Zinn)

☙

Parenting is a giant responsibility forever, so we need to learn how to drop the guilt and go easy on ourselves when we mess up. (Rachael Bermingham)

Parenting is a life time job and does not stop when a child grows up. (Jake Slope)

Parenting is an impossible job at any age. (Harrison Ford)

Parenting is not for sissies. You have to sacrifice and grow up. (Jillian M)

Parenting is one of the best management training programs there is. (Irene Rosenfeld)

Parenting is really just a matter of tracking, of hoping your kids do not get so far ahead you can no longer see their next moves. (Jodi Picoult)

Parenting is the easiest thing in the world to have an opinion about but the hardest thing in the world to do. (Anne Lamoti)

Parenting is the greatest pay it forward system on earth. We don't owe our parents anything. We owe our children everything. The same was true for our parents. The same will be true for our children. (Dan Pearce)

Parenting requires a delicate balance of letting your child be your spiritual teacher while you maintain the clarity and boundaries to be her Earthly teacher. (Jennifer Griffin)

Parenting should be a passion, not a part-time pursuit. (Ellen Hopkins)

Parenting today is very different from what our parents or grandparents experienced. Some of us may recall growing up in a home where Dad was present, and his word was law. (Elaine D)

Parenting without a sense of humour is like being an accountant who sucks at math. (Amber Dusick)

Parents are living gods. They do everything to make their children happy and expect nothing in return. (SK Murugan)

Parents can only give good advice or put them on the right paths, but the final forming of a person's character lies in their own hands. (Anne Frank)

Parents can tell but never teach, unless they practise what they preach. (Arnold H Glasow)

Parents forgive their children least readily for the faults they themselves instilled in them. (Marie VE)

Parents have the glorious opportunity of being the most powerful influence, above and beyond any other, on the new lives that bless their homes. (LT Perry)

Parents know all about the verses related to how children should behave but not so much about those that remind them about how they should behave. (Jeff VanVonderen)

Parents need to fill a child's bucket of self-esteem so high that the rest of the world can't poke enough holes to drain it dry. (Alvin Price)

৪০

Parents need to realize that comparison is not motivation. (Anon)

৪০

Parents pin all their hopes and dreams on their children, and as a result, those kids feel all kinds of pressure to be some sort of familial saviour destined to achieve greatness and keep their extended family from drowning. (Aaron H Aceves)

৪০

Parents should not smoke in order to discourage their kids from smoking. A child is more likely to smoke when they have been raised in the environment of a smoker. (Christy T)

৪০

Parents were the only ones obligated to love you; from the rest of the world you had to earn it. (Ann Brashares)

৪০

Parents wonder why the streams are bitter, when tehy themselves have poisoned the fountain. (John Locke)

৪০

Peer pressure becomes more powerful when our children are away from our influence and when their defences are weakened late at night. If you have ever felt uneasy about an overnight activity, don't be afraid to respond to that warning voice inside. Always be prayerful when it comes to protecting your precious children. (Larry R. Lawrence)

৪০

People expect you to change when you become a mother, and of course my priorities changed when I had Violet. She is number one in my life and the best thing that ever happened to me, but I still have fun, I am still myself, but that is made out to seem like I am rebelling against motherhood. (Imelda May)

☙

Permissiveness is the principle of treating children as if they were adults; and the tactic of making sure they never reach that stage.(Thomas Szasz)

☙

Play helps build a warm relationship between family members and create a bank of positive feelings and experiences that can be drawn upon in times of conflict. Through play, you can help your children solve problems, test out ideas, and explore their imaginations.(Carolyn Webster-Stratton)

☙

Please do not treat your child like a performing animal. Treat her like a unique individual to be loved and cherished.(Ramendra Kumar)

☙

Please remember children can read between the lines and beyond the words. (Ramendra Kumar)

☙

Poor communication is inherited from parents or family members. They never talked about feelings, they yelled. They held onto secrets because they did not want to make things awkward. Break that toxic chain. (GL Lambert)

☙

Praise your children openly, reprove them secretly. (William Cecil)

☙

Raise your children to love and embrace others. Tell them they are beautiful, they may grow up to be stars one day, and beautiful will never mean as much in a magazine as it will come from you. (Kaiden Blake)

☙

Raising children is like baking cookies at high altitudes. The recipe doesn't work. You must open the oven door and keep checking on the cookies. (Dr Margaret Aranda)

☙

Raising kids is part joy and part guerilla warfare. (Ed Asner)

❧

Raising people is not some lark. It's serious work with serious repercussions. It's air-traffic control. You can't step out for a minute; you can barely pause to scratch your ankle. (Kelly Corrigan)

❧

Reading aloud with children is known to be the single most important activity for building the knowledge and skills they will eventually require for learning to read. (Marilyn Jager Adams)

❧

Reading makes kids more intelligent. It does not just make them seem more intelligent, reading creates new neural connections in a child's brain by stimulating the growth of new neurons as they imagine the world the writer has put on paper.(Jackie French)

❧

Reading to babies is like hugging them with words. (Sheree Fitch)

❧

Reading to children opens their minds and fills their hearts. (Jacqui Shepherd)

❧

Reading to children...gives them more of exactly what they need : more loving adult attention, more language, more opportunities to experience mutual engagement and empathy. (Meghan Cox Gurdon)

❧

Relationships are built on small, consistent deposits of time. You can't cram for what's most important. If you want to connect with your kids, you've got to be available consistently, not randomly. (Andy Stanley)

❧

Remember, the goal is not to raise great kids, it is to raise kids who become great adults. (Andy Andrews)

☙

Remember, you are not managing an inconvenience; You are raising a human being. (Kittie Frantz)

☙

Resolution, like responsibility, is a product of ownership, and kids can't resolve a conflict until they figure out how they contributed to it. (Richard Eyre)

☙

Respecting a child teaches them that even the smallest, most powerless, most vulnerable person is worthy of respect. And that is a lesson our world desperately needs to learn. (LR Knost)

☙

Respond to your children with love in their worst moments, their broken moments, their angry moments, their selfish moments, their lonely moments, their frustrated moments, their inconvenient moments, because it is in their most unlovable human moments that they most need to feel loved. (LR Knost)

☙

Reward your kids with things they get to do instead of things they get to have. This teaches them that true happiness comes from experiences instead of possessions.(Anon)

☙

Saturday mornings, I have learned, are a great opportunity for kids to sneak into your bed, fall back asleep, and kick you in the face. (Dan Pearce)

☙

Say 'no' only when it really matters. Wear a bright red shirt with bright orange shorts? Sure. Put water in the toy tea set? Okay. Sleep with your head at the foot of the bed? Fine. (Gretchen Rubin)

☙

Saying no to your children can be an act of love. (Frank Sonnenberg)

ॐ

Screaming at children over their grades, especially to the point of the child's tears, is child abuse, pure and simple. It's not funny and it's not good parenting. It is a crushing, scarring, disastrous experience for the child. It isn't the least bit funny. (Ben Stein)

ॐ

Self-reflection – based on experiences, principles and goals that we have gathered across our lifetime – allows us to course-correct. This is constantly required as we muddle along, gradually learning better ways for us to parent over time. (Leon Levitt)

ॐ

Setting a good example for your children takes all the fun out of middle age. (William Feather)

ॐ

Setting boundaries isn't an alternative to loving your child. It is a means of loving her. (Henry Cloud)

ॐ

Show your teachers ungrudging respect and your children unfeigned love. (Marcus Aurelius)

ॐ

Single moms: You are a doctor, a teacher, a nurse, a maid, a cook, a referee, a heroine, a provider, a defender, a protector, a true Superwoman. Wear your cape proudly. (Mandy Hale)

ॐ

So much is asked of parents, and so little is given. (Virginia Satir)

ॐ

So often, children are punished for being human. They are not allowed to have grumpy moods, bad days, disrespectful tones, or bad attitudes. Yet, we adults have them all the time. None of us are perfect. We must stop holding our children to a higher standard of perfection than we can attain ourselves. (Rebecca Eanes)

❧

Some parents pin all their hopes and dreams on their children, and as a result, those kids feel all kinds of pressure to be some sort of familial saviour destined to achieve greatness and keep their extended family from drowning. (Aaron H Aceves)

❧

Someday my children will look fondly on the annoying things I did and see them clearly as evidence of love. (Richelle E. Goodrich)

❧

Sometimes being a good parent means knowing when to let go. (Liz Braswell)

❧

Sometimes kids want you to hurt the way they hurt. (Mitch Albom)

❧

Sometimes the strength of motherhood is greater than natural laws. (Barbara K)

❧

Somewhere along the line we stopped trying to fix the child that we had expected and started to enjoy the child that was. (Meg Blomfield)

❧

Spending Quality time doesn't mean merely sharing physical space, it means attention, involvement and sharing of emotional space. (Ramendra Kumar)

❧

Stop taking life and yourselves so seriously. Just let go and allow the child in you to take over and ENJOY! (Ramendra Kumar)

❧

Sublimating your desire for activities that don't involve your children does not make you a more impressive parent; it just makes you a more exhausted and resentful one. (Charlie Warzel)

Successful mothers are not the ones that never struggled. They are the ones that never give up despite the struggles. (Sharon Jaynes)

Surround her with a village of aunties, women who have qualities you would like her to admire. Talk about how much you admire them. Children copy and learn my example. Talk about what you admire about them. (CN Adichie)

Taking care of myself makes me a better mom because I parent from abundance, not lack thereof. (Lauren Tamm)

Teach your kids that someone not liking them is not an indication they need to try harder or change who they are to gain approval. It is not our job to make other people like us. It is our job to like ourselves. (Christine Derengowski)

Teaching a child from a young age, through words and actions, that every human being's life and safety is precious and is to be guarded promotes a culture of nonviolence. (Mike Weiford)

That was another nice thing about my parents. There was none of that holding on to knowledge and power that some parents go in for. We were all adults together, on a plateau of equality. (Julian Barnes)

That's what children are for—that their parents may not be bored. (Ivan Turgenev)

The absolute best way to raise kind kids is to be kind parents. (Galit Breen)

The beauty of motherhood is not in the freshly pressed shirts and smiling photos we show the world. The beauty of motherhood is in the folds and creases of our lives, the grimaces and tantrums, the moments when we have to grit our teeth to get through, when we pound on windows and yell and scream and demand better of each other and ourselves. (Robyn Pasante)

The beauty that surrounds me is absolutely breathtaking, it is the faces of my children. (Anabela L)

The best advice my mom has ever given me is to never give up. She believes when one door shuts, another door opens. Always, always move forward. (Melissa Rivers)

The best inheritance a parent can give his children is a few minutes of his time each day. (OA Battista)

The best parenting strives to educate children in how to live -- enthusiastically, compassionately, without greed, striving for a better world. (David R. Wommack)

The best security blanket a child can have is parents who respect each other. (Janet Blaustone)

The best teachers are those who show you where to look, but don't tell youwhat to see. (Alexander K Trenfor)

The best thing you can do for your kids is to stop doing so much for them. Teach them how to clean their own space, do their own laundry, make their own food and think for themselves. They will thank you someday. (Brooke Hampton)

&

The best toy a child can have is a parent who gets down on the floor and plays with them. (Bruce Perry)

&

The best way to give advice to your children is to find out what they want and then advise them to do it. (Harry S Truman)

&

The best way to guide children without coercion is to be ourselves. (Madeleine L'Engle)

&

The best way to keep children at home is to make the home atmosphere pleasant, and let the air out of the tires. (Dorothy Parker)

&

The best way to make children good is to make them happy. (Oscar Wilde)

&

The challenging part of parenting for me is to make sure that an individual person is an individual and not some sort of cookie-cutter version of me. At the same time, I want to make sure that I impart my sense of the world as an adult. (Jamie Lee Curtis)

&

The child who gets distracted by observing a feather on the ground and hearing the wind rustle leaves will grow to understand so much more. (Angela A)

&

The child will not learn to trust someone weaker than himself or herself. If they can control and manipulate the adult, they are stronger. The adult must be strong enough to be in charge in a loving way for the child to learn to trust and bond. (Nancy L Thomas)

❧

The children who need love the most will always ask for it in the most unloving ways. (Russel Barkley)

❧

The commonest fallacy among women is that simply having children makes them a mother-which is as absurd as believing that having a piano makes one a musician. (Sydney J Harris)

❧

The danger of motherhood. You relive your early self, through the eyes of your mother. (Joyce Carol Oates)

❧

The difference between punishment and discipline is a powerful child. (Danny Silk)

❧

The easiest way to get your children to listen to you and to learn from you, is by connecting with them first. (Carolina King)

❧

The Golden Rule of Parenting is do unto your children as you wish your parents had done unto you! (Louise Hart)

❧

The goodness of the mother is written in the gaiety of the child. (Victor Hugo)

❧

The greatest challenge of parenting is in the inner work it requires: the strength and confidence in believing that we are not in control of, but the answer for our children.(Kelly Bartlett)

❧

The greatest gift a parent can give a child is self-confidence. (Stewart Stafford)

ॐ

The greatest possessions I leave for my children are books. (Lailah Gifty Akita)

ॐ

The hardest job kids face today is learning good manners without seeing any. (Fred Astaire)

ॐ

The interesting thing about being a mother is that everyone wants pets, but no one but me cleans the kitty litter. (Meryl Streep)

ॐ

The life of a mother is the life of a child, you are two blossoms on a single branch. (Karen M Miller)

ॐ

The metaphor of transformation deepens as we consider how a butterfly needs to struggle for its ability to fly. If the chrysalis is broken by someone in an attempt to help free the butterfly, its wings will be shrivelled and immobile.(Gabriel Cousens)

ॐ

The miracle of children is that we just don't know how they will change or who they will become. (Eileen KM)

ॐ

The more people have studied different methods of bringing up children the more they have come to the conclusion that what good mothers and fathers instinctively feel like doing for their babies is the best after all. (Benjamin Spock)

ॐ

The more you test him, the slower he will learn and the less he'll want to do. The less you test him, the quicker he will learn and the more he'll want to learn. Knowledge is the most precious gift you can give your child. Give it as generously as you give him food. (Glenn Doman)

❧

The most beautiful sight in the world is a little child going confidently down the road of life after you have shown him the way. (Confucius)

❧

The most important gifts we can give our children are confidence in their ability to remake themselves again and again and the tools with which to do that job. (Anders Ericsson)

❧

The most important thing a father can do for his children is to love their mother. (T Hesburgh)

❧

The most important thing that parents can teach their children is how to get along without them. (Frank A Clark)

❧

The most powerful way to change the world is to live in front of our children the way we would like the world to be. (Graham White)

❧

The most profound thing we can offer our children is our own healing. (Anne Lamott)

❧

The mother-child relationship is paradoxical and, in a sense, tragic. It requires the most intense love on the mother's side, yet this very love must help the child grow away from the mother, and to become fully independent. (Erich Fromm)

❧

The natural state of motherhood is unselfishness. When you become a mother, you are no longer the center of your own universe. You relinquish that position to your children. (Jessica Lange)

The newborn has only three demands. They are warmth in the arms of its mother, food from her breasts, and security in the knowledge of her presence. Breastfeeding satisfies all three. (Grantly Dick-Read)

The object of education is to prepare the young to educate themselves throughout their lives. (Robert M Hutchins)

The one who plants trees, knowing that he or she will never sit in their shade, has at least started to understand the meaning of life. (R Tagore)

The only person that knows how to parent your child is you. Trust your instincts. (Carolina King)

The parents exist to teach the child, but also they must learn what the child has to teach them, and the child has a very great deal to teach them. (Arnold Bennett)

The point of parenting is not to have all the answers before we start out but instead to figure it out on the go as our children grow. Because as they do, so will we. (Bridgett Miller)

The raising of a child is the building of a cathedral. You can't cut corners. (Dave Eggers)

The real menace in dealing with a five-year old is that in no time at all you begin to sound like a five-year-old. (Jean Kerr)

The reality is that most of us communicate the same way that we grew up. That communication style becomes our normal way of dealing with issues, our blueprint for communication. It's what we know and pass on to our own children. We either become our childhood or we make a conscious choice to change it. (Kristen Crockett)

☙

The reason why kids are crazy is because nobody can face the responsibility of bringing them up. (John Lennon)

☙

The secret of dealing successfully with a child is not to be its parent. (Mell Lazarus)

☙

The thing about parenting rules is there are not any. That is what makes it so difficult. (Ewan McGregor)

☙

The three-year-old is not an incomplete five-year-old ; the child is not an incomplete adult. Never are we simply on our way, we have arrived. (Joseph Chilton Pearce)

☙

The value of marriage is not that adults produce children, but that children produce adults. (Peter De Vries)

☙

The very fact that you worry about being a good mom means that you are one. (Jodi Picoult)

☙

The voice of parents is the voice of gods, for to their children they are heaven's lieutenants. (William Shakespeare)

☙

The way kids learn to make good decisions is by making decisions, not by following directions.(Alfie Kohn)

❧

The way we speak to our child matters, for those words travel beyond their ears, settling into the creases of their hearts and the crevices of their self-worth. (Anon)

❧

The way we talk to our children becomes their inner voice. (Peggy O'Mara)

❧

The well-being and welfare of children should always be our focus. (Todd Tiahrt)

❧

There are only two lasting bequests we can hope to give our children. One of these is root, the other, wings. (Goethe)

❧

There are so many quiet times you spend as a mother that are not glorified but are a foundation for your kids. No matter what, there was always a thick safety net under the trapeze. (Tina Fey)

❧

There are times as a parent when you realize that your job is not to be the parent you always imagined you would be, the parent you always wished you had. Your job is to be the parent your child needs, given the particulars of his or her own life and nature. (Ayelet Waldman)

❧

There is a lot of talk these days about giving children self-esteem. It is not something you can give. It is something they have to build. (Randy Pausch)

❧

There is no friendship, no love, like that of the parent for the child. (Henry Ward Beecher)

❧

There is no greater good in all the world than motherhood. The influence of a mother in the lives of her children is beyond calculation. (James E Faust)

❧

There is no school equal to a decent home and no teacher equal to a virtuous parent. (Mahatma Gandhi)

❧

There is no single effort more radical in its potential for saving the world than a transformation of the way we raise our children. (Marianne W)

❧

There is no single greater contribution in the infinite game than to raise children who will continue to grow and serve others long after we are gone. To live a life with an infinite mindset means thinking about the second and third order effects of our decisions. (Simon Sinek)

❧

There is no substitute for books in the life of a child. (Mary Ellen Chase)

❧

There is no such thing as being the perfect parent. So just be a real one. (Sue Atkins)

❧

There is no way to be a perfect mother and a million ways to be a good one. (Jill Churchill)

❧

There is nothing more dangerous than a lazy parent. (Wes Fesler)

❧

There is nothing that moves a loving father's soul quite like his child's cry. (Joni E Tada)

❧

There will be so many times you feel like you have failed. But in the eyes, heart and mind of your child, you are Super Mom. (Stephanie P)

There's no single effort more radical in it's potential for saving the world than a transformation of the way we raise our children. (Marianne Williamson)

They show you the path, they take you along, choose friends right to make life bright. (Vasantha K Dandem)

Through the blur, I wondered if I was alone or if other parents felt the same way I did - that everything involving our children was painful in some way. The emotions, whether they were joy, sorrow, love or pride, were so deep and sharp that in the end they left you raw, exposed and yes, in pain. The human heart was not designed to beat outside the human body and yet, each child represented just that - a parent's heart bared, beating forever outside its chest. (Debra Ginsberg)

Throughout our parenting life, the greatest battle is not with the child but with our own worries. (Leon Levitt)

To all mothers in every circumstance, including those who struggle, I say, "Be peaceful, Believe in God and yourself. You are doing better than you think you are." (Elder JL Holland)

To all you parents out there, don't make your little girls, or little boys, so thirsty for love that they will want to drink water that will poison them. (Lisa Bedrick)

To be in your children's memories tomorrow, you have to be in their lives today. (Barbara Johnson)

To have a child is to voluntarily bare one's soul to the angst that arises when we love another human being more than we love ourselves, and then we work to launch them into a world that does not. (Craig D Lounsbrough)

ജ

To maintain a joyful family requires much from both the parents and the children. Each member of the family has to become, in a special way, the servant of the others. (Pope John Paul II)

ജ

To me luxury is to be at home with my daughter, and the occasional massage does not hurt. (Olivia NJ)

ജ

To me, parenting is all about trust. If you don't live by your words or actions, how do you expect your kids to listen to you? (Kevin Heath)

ജ

To my children, I am sorry for the unhealed parts of me that in turn hurt you. It was never a lack of love for you. Only a lack of love for myself. (Teresa Shanti)

ജ

To nurture your connections, hug your family members daily, have conversations, and share loving, supportive and positive things about each other. (Tara Bianca)

ജ

To you who are parents, I say, show love to your children. You know you love them, but make certain they know it as well. They are so precious. Let them know. Call upon our Heavenly Father for help as you care for their needs each day and as you deal with the challenges which inevitably come with parenthood. You need more than your own wisdom in rearing them. (Thomas SM)

ജ

Too bad for any parent who has become accustomed to ruling by force, because at some point the kids just get too big to slap around. (Barbara

Ehrenreich)

Too many parents fail to understand that there is a difference between fitting in and being liked, that there is a difference between being normal and being happy. High school is temporary, family is not. (Alexandra Robbins)

Too much love never spoils children. Children become spoiled when we substitute presents for presence. (Anthony Withman)

Treat a child as though he already is the person he is capable of becoming. (Haim Ginott)

Uselessness, she thought, was the permanent condition of parenthood. (Lisa Unger)

Using fear to change behaviour does not work because children cannot learn when they are afraid.(Anon)

View your child as a beautiful creation of God and empathise with her. However small she may be she has a right to express her opinion and reach out to you. (Ramendra Kumar)

We all need a cheering committee and parents are a child's most important fans. (Vivian Kirkfield)

We are apt to forget that children watch examples better than they listen to preaching. (Roy L Smith)

We are branches of the same tree, we share chocolates, we pull daggers, love and hate come to us naturally and you call it rivalry ! (Vasantha K Dandem)

৪৩

We are doing the best we can, so it would be really nice if moms supported each other instead of pointing out the flaws. We are all trying to do the best we can. (Jana Kramer)

৪৩

We are imperfect humans growing imperfect humans i an imperfect world, and that is perfectly okay. (LR Knost)

৪৩

We are the windows through which our children first see the world. Let us be conscious of the view. (Katrina Kenison)

৪৩

We do not develop habits of genuine love automatically. We learn by watching effective role models- most specifically by observing how our parents express love for each other day in and day out. (Josh McDowell)

৪৩

We don't always do the things our parents want us to do, but it is their mistake if they can't find a way to love us anyway. (J Courtney Sullivan)

৪৩

We have such a brief opportunity to pass on to our children our love for this Earth, and to tell our stories. These are the moments when the world is made whole. In my children's memories, the adventures we've had together in nature will always exist. (Richard Louv)

৪৩

We have to learn to remind the other parents who think we're being careless when we loosen our grip that we are actually trying to teach our children how to get along in the world, and that we believe this is our job. A child who can fend for himself is a lot safer than one forever coddled, because the coddled child will not have Mom or Dad around all the time, even though they act as if he will. (Lenore Skenazy)

❧

We may not be able to prepare the future for our children, but we can at least prepare our children for the future. (FD Roosevelt)

❧

We must focus on reality and what our kids tell us about ourselves, which is that what they really want and need is more of what we do best-talk, encourage, and spend time with them. (Meg Meeker)

❧

We must imbue our children with principles of the higher-self, principles which see all people as true equals, and above all, which are sensitive to the delicate and fragile balance of life. (Bryant McGil)

❧

We must remember that one day our children are going to follow our example instead of our advice. (Carolina King)

❧

We must return to optimism in our parenting. To focus on the joys, not the hassles; the love, not the disappointments; the common sense, not the complexities. (Fred G. Gosman)

❧

We never know the love of a parent till we become parents ourselves. (HW Beecher)

❧

We spend the first 12 months of our children's lives teaching them to walk and talk and the next 12 months teaching them to sit down and shut up. (Phyllis Diller)

❧

We teach children to colour inside the lines, and then expect adults to think outside the box. (Anon)

❧

We, as parents, are to bless our children so our children want to make the choices in this world that lead them to victorious living. (Anne Weaver)

❧

What a child does not receive he can seldom later give. (PD James)

❧

What a difference it makes to come home to a child. (Margaret Fuller)

❧

What is done to children, they will do to society. (Karl Meninger)

❧

What it is like to be a parent : it is one of the hardest things you will ever do but in exchange it teaches you the meaning of unconditional love. (Nicholas Sparks)

❧

What parent has it easy? I just never make the difficulty of it an obstacle. I just do it. (Marlee Marlin)

❧

What we do today, will impact who our children will be tomorrow. (Carolina King)

❧

What we sometimes see as annoying, incessant questions from a child may be a plea for recognition. Maybe they do not need an answer as much as attention.(Dr. Rand Olson)

❧

what your personality is like, you will always be Al Gore to your wife's Bill Clinton. She feels the pain and you are the annoying nerd telling them to turn off the lights. (Jim Gaffigan)

❧

When a child believes there is something wrong with them due to criticism, expectations, or judgements, they turn against themselves and experience the ultimate separation. (Tara Bianca)

ॐ

When a child can't calm down. They need connection and comfort, not criticism and control. (Jane Evans)

ॐ

When a child gives you a gift, even if it is a rock they just picked up, exude gratitude. It might be the only thing they have to give, and they have chosen to give it to you. (Dean Jackson C)

ॐ

When a child hits a child, we call it aggression. When a child hits an adult, we call it hostility. When an adult hits an adult, we call it assault. When an adult hits a child, we call it discipline. (Haim Ginott)

ॐ

When a flower does not bloom, you fix the environment in which it grows, not the flower. (Alexander Den Heijer)

ॐ

When a teacher reads aloud, it is a bonding between the teacher, the children, the books, and the act of reading.(Lester Laminack)

ॐ

When correcting a child, the goal is to apply light, not heat. (Woodrow Wilson)

ॐ

When my child makes a mistake and I feel tempted to scold them, I try to remember how I want to be treated when I make mistakes in my own life..with compassion, curiosity and grace.(Shelly Robinson)

ॐ

When parents see their children's problems as opportunities to build the relationship instead of as negative, burdensome irritations, it totally changes the nature of parent-child interaction. Parents become more willing, even excited, about deeply understanding and helping their children. (Stephen R Covey)

∾

When the world comes for your children with the knives out, it is your job to stand in the way. (Joe Hill)

∾

When they are little you are the hero, when they grow up you are a monster and when they are old you are their pride! —Metamorphosis of Parenthood. (Dr Lucas D Shallua)

∾

When we choose to be parents, we accept another human being as part of ourselves, and a large part of our emotional selves will stay with that person as long as we live. From that time on, there will be another person on this earth whose orbit around us will affect us as surely as the moon affects the tides, and affect us in some ways more deeply than anyone else can. Our children are extensions of ourselves. (Fred Rogers)

∾

When we learn to seek validation from our parents and the outside world, it is easy to fall for the idea that if we just fit in, look good enough for others, or achieve great success, all will be right in the world. (Tara Bianca)

∾

When you have children, suddenly the world seems such a terrifying place. Every stick and stone, every car, every animal, Christ, every person, is suddenly a terrible threat. You realise you'd do anything, anything, to keep them safe: steal, like, kill, you name it. But sometimes there just isn't anything you can do. And that's the hardest thing. (Elly Griffiths)

∾

When you hold your baby in your arms the first time, and you think of all the things you can say and do to influence him, it is a tremendous responsibility. What you do with him can influence not only him , but everyone he meets and not for a day or a month or a year but for time and eternity. (Rose Kennedy)

When you take the time to actually listen, with humility, to what people have to say, it's amazing what you can learn. Especially if the people who are doing the talking also happen to be children. (Greg Mortenson)

When you win the child wins, when you lose you both lose. (Nancy L Thomas)

When your child is acting up, remember that they are probably just trying to get your attention. Fill up their love bucket before you do anything else.(Carolina King)

When your children are tennagers, it is important to have a dog so that someone in the house is happy to see you. (Nora Ephron)

Where did we ever get the crazy idea that in order to make children do better, first we have to make them feel worse? Think of the last time you felt humiliated or treated unfairly. Did you feel like cooperating or doing better? (Jane Nelson)

Where parents do too much for their children, the children will not do much for themselves.(Elbert Hubbard)

Whether or not you have children yourself, you are a parent to the next generation. If we can only stop thinking of children as individual property and think of them as the next generation, then we can realize we all have a role to play. (Charlotte SK)

Whether you're explaining where pets go when they die or teaching your child to recycle, your philosophies have ramifications. For the rest of history, echoes of your voice will be heard. (Beth Ann Fennelly)

જી

While I was drying off Maddie after her bath tonight, she said, I love you, to me for the first time. It sounded like, All lub boo, but I did not care. To reciprocate, I showed her what an ex-Marine looks like when he cries. (Jim Beaver)

જી

While we try to teach our children all about life, Our children teach us what life is all about. (Angela Schwindt)

જી

With children the clock is reset. We forget what came before. (Jhumpa Lahiri)

જી

Yelling silences your message. Speak quietly so children can hear your words instead of just your voice. (LR Knost)

જી

You are not just equal to A or A+, you are a human, much more than that. Life does not start or end with grades. We love you anytime with all your hearts. (Vasantha K Dandem)

જી

You are the bows from which your children as living arrows are sent forth. (Khalil Gibran)

જી

You are the gatekeeper of your child's mental diet. (Gary Chapman)

જી

You can learn many things from children. How much patience you have, for instance. (FP Adams)

જી

You can't cling to the side your whole life, that one lesson every parent needs to teach a child is "If you don't want to sink, you better figure out how to swim. (Jeannette Walls)

You can't teach children to behave better by making them feel worse. When children feel better they behave better. (Pam Lee)

You can't make your kids do anything. All you can do is make them wish they had. And then, they will make you wish you hadn't made them wish they had. (Marshall B. Rosenberg)

You do not have to make your children into wonderful people. You just have to remind them that they are wonderful people. (William Martin)

You do not have to raise children. You have to give them space, love and support to grow. Every human being is capable of a unique possibility. (Sadhguru Jaggi Vasudev)

You don't gain authority by raising your voice. You prove you don't have any. (Benjamin Lotter)

You have a lifetime to work, but children are only young once. (Polish proverb)

You learn so much about yourself from being a parent and you care more about the world you are raising your kids in. (Kim Kardashian)

You love your child for who the child is, not as an extension of your identity or as an example of your good parenting or even as a companion. (Robert

Fritz)

∞

You may have had a parent that judged you or was highly critical. If so, you may be so familiar with judgement directed at you during your formative years that you automatically judge yourself. (Tara Bianca)

∞

You must first teach a child he is loved. Only then is he ready to learn everything else.(Amanda Morgan)

∞

You start to focus less on what's wrong for you and more on what is wrong for the next generation. It mobilises you. Some moms channel that into the PTA, and other moms channel it into marching for women's rights, so moms need to be more rebellious than ever. (Pink)

∞

You try as a parent. You love beyond reason. You fight beyond endurance. You hope beyond despair. You never think, until the very last moment, that it still might not be enough. (Lisa Gardner)

∞

You will love your children far more than you ever loved your parents, and - in the recognition that your own children cannot fathom the depth of your love- you come to understand the tragic, unrequited love of your own parents. (Ursula Hegi)

∞

You will never have this day with your children again. Tomorrow, they will be a little older than they were today. This day is a gift. Just breathe, notice, smell and touch them, study their faces and little feet. Pay attention. Relish the charms of the present.Enjoy today. It will be over before you know it. (Jen Hatmaker)

∞

You will teach them to fly, but they will not fly your flight. You will teach them to dream, but they will not dream your dream. You will teach them to live, but they will not live your life. Nevertheless, in every flight, in every life, in every dream, the print of the way you taught them will remain. (Mother Teresa)

You'll sacrifice for your child in ways you had never imagined. And they're not exciting and earth shattering ways, either. They're small, seemingly insignificant gestures that mean the world to them. (Heather McVea)

Young children especially need the visual reinforcement of seeing you turn to Scripture for wisdom. (Kara Durbin)

Your beauty lies inside, you are more worthy than your attire, you are already a marvel, you don't need somebody's approval. (Vasantha K Dandem)

Your children are the greatest gift God will give to you, and their souls the heaviest responsibility He will place in your hands. Take time with them, teach them to have faith in God. Be a person in whom they can have faith. When you are old, nothing else you've done will have mattered as much. (Lisa Wingate)

Your children need your presence more than your presents.(Jesse Jackson)

Your children vividly remember every unkind thing you ever did to them, plus a few you really did not. (Mignon McLaughlin)

Your children will become what you are, so be what you want them to be. (David Bly)

Your children will remember how you made them feel whether those feelings are good or bad. And they will remember the words you used. (AE Rogers)

જી

Your greatest contribution to the universe may not be something you do, but someone you raise. (Anon)

જી

Your kids require you most of all to love them for who they are, not to spend your whole time trying to correct them. (Bill Ayers)

જી

Your words as a parent have great power. Use them wisely and make sure tehy come from the heart. (Carolina King)

જી

AUTHOR CAN BE REACHED AT GORASK@GMAIL.COM

III
Notes